I0796699

POUR DECISIONS

Pour Decisions

13-Digit ISBN: 978-1-40035-283-8
10-Digit ISBN: 1-40035-283-5

Books published by Cider Mill Press Book Publishers are available at special discounts for bulk purchases in the United States by corporations, institutions, and other organizations. For more information, please contact the publisher.

Cider Mill Press Book Publishers
"Where good books are ready for press"
501 Nelson Place
Nashville, Tennessee 37214, USA

cidermillpress.com

HarperCollins Publishers, Macken House, 39/40 Mayor Street Upper, Dublin 1, D01 C9W8, Ireland (https://www.harpercollins.com)

Typography: Bembo Std, Degular Mono, Morning Memories Script Alt, Vincente

Image Credits: Photos on pages 17, 30, 34, 45, 46, 107, 125, 144, 156, 159, 163, 167, 170, 172, 181, 185, 187, 189, and 209 courtesy of Cider Mill Press. Photos on pages 56, 59, and 61 by Emanuele Mensah. All other images used under official license from Shutterstock.com.

Printed in Bosnia & Herzegovina
25 26 27 28 29 GPS 5 4 3 2 1

First Edition

POUR DECISIONS

100 cocktails inspired by your ex

contents

INTRODUCTION

Love is a cocktail: intoxicating, unpredictable, and liable to make you feel terrible afterward if you're not careful. This book is a toast to the ones who broke our hearts, lit our phones on fire, or simply disappeared mid-brunch with no explanation. We've all had at least one—*that* ex. Maybe they were charming in public and chaos in private. Maybe they ghosted you after introducing you to their mother. Or maybe they just weren't worth your considerable time and effort.

We're here to help you move on—because nothing says healing like mixing the perfect cocktail while muttering their name under your breath. From tequila-fueled disasters to whiskey-fueled nostalgia, we've turned every emotional train wreck into something worth sipping. These drinks aren't just recipes; they're revenge fantasies in a glass. They're the spicy comebacks you wish you'd delivered and the closure you never got—but way more fun and significantly more garnished.

So whether you're drinking to forget, drinking to remember, or just here to enjoy a good cocktail, welcome. You've found the ultimate breakup bar cart. Here's to the ones who taught us what we *don't* want—and to the spirits that helped us survive them.

SELECTING YOUR SPIRITS

Let's get one thing straight: If you won't settle for less in your dating life, your liquor shelf should be no different. Sure, heartbreak may have left you emotionally bankrupt, but that doesn't mean your cocktails have to taste like regret and rubbing alcohol. Quality matters—because the only thing worse than crying into a drink is crying into a *bad* one. Whether you're mixing for friends or just for yourself on a Tuesday night, your spirits deserve to be as bold, complex, and well-chosen as your next rebound.

That said, we get it—sometimes your wallet's feeling as empty as your DMs. If you're on a budget, vodka's your best bet; it will rarely betray you when you go bottom shelf. Cheap gin is basically a botanical betrayal, and bad whiskey? That's regret waiting to happen. But remember: "Inexpensive" isn't the same as "undrinkable." There are some solid go-to bottles out there that won't cost you your dignity or your taste buds. See our list here for some ideas! And keep an eye on your local distilleries; they just might surprise you with something special.

VODKA

BUDGET: SVEDKA

CLASSIC: SKYY

PERFECT: GREY GOOSE

RUM

BUDGET: BACARDI

CLASSIC: CAPTAIN MORGAN

PERFECT: EL DORADO

GIN

BUDGET: SEAGRAM'S

CLASSIC: TANQUERAY

PERFECT: BOMBAY SAPPHIRE

TEQUILA

BUDGET: AGAVALES

CLASSIC: JOSE CUERVO

PERFECT: 1800

WHISKEY

BUDGET: EVAN WILLIAMS

CLASSIC: MAKER'S MARK

PERFECT: WOODFORD RESERVE

MUST-HAVE MIXERS

TRIPLE SEC

SWEET VERMOUTH

LIME JUICE

LEMON JUICE

BITTERS

GRENADINE

SIMPLE SYRUP (SEE BELOW)

NICE-TO-HAVE MIXERS

DRY VERMOUTH

CRÈME DE MENTHE

COCONUT RUM

CAMPARI

ORGEAT SYRUP

FLAVORED BITTERS

simple syrup

Place 1 cup sugar and 1 cup water in a saucepan and bring it to a boil, stirring to dissolve the sugar. Remove the pan from heat and let the syrup cool completely before using or storing.

BAR TOOLS

Much like dating, making a great cocktail requires a mix of charm, timing, and having the right tools so you don't completely embarrass yourself. Sure, some drinks are as easy as pouring and pretending everything's fine, but others require a little more effort (and maybe some emotional support). That's where bar tools come in. Here's what we recommend having on hand.

MUST-HAVES

COCKTAIL SHAKER

STRAINER

JIGGER

KNIFE

BOTTLE OPENER

CORKSCREW

NICE TO HAVE

COCKTAIL STIRRER

MUDDLER

JUICER

ZESTER

GLASSWARE

Can't drink without a glass! But you can always drink out of a different glass than the kind we recommend if you need or want to—just be sure to adjust the serving size accordingly, especially if your glass is smaller than the one we suggest.

MUST-HAVES	NICE TO HAVE	WISH LIST
PINT GLASS	MARGARITA GLASS	HURRICANE GLASS
SHOT GLASS	COCKTAIL GLASS	DAIQUIRI GLASS
ROCKS GLASS	CHAMPAGNE FLUTE	IRISH COFFEE GLASS
HIGHBALL GLASS	MASON JAR	SOUR GLASS

Now it's time to move on—to the cocktails, of course. Each chapter in this book is centered around a different spirit. Because let's be honest: Some hard truths go down easier with vodka, while others demand the dark poetry of whiskey. These drinks are designed to match the mood, the memory, and the sheer mess of it all. Enjoy them on your own, or throw a party with your friends, where you each bring a batch of drinks and your worst dating horror stories to share.

Ready to stir up old memories, shake them off, and toast to learning from our mistakes? It's time to make some *Pour Decisions*.

Situationship, page 20

TEQUI-LIE TO ME

Just like a messy ex, tequila knows how to turn up the heat, loosen the truth, and leave you questioning your life choices the next morning. This chapter is a salute to the heartbreaks that burned going down but somehow left you coming back for more. Whether you're here for the salt-rimmed tears or the lime-squeezed memories, these cocktails pack a punch worthy of the wild ride.

INGREDIENTS

1 oz. tequila

1 splash grapefruit juice

1 lime wedge (juiced)

2 oz. grapefruit soda

1 grapefruit wheel (garnish)

GLASSWARE

Highball glass

The dreaded 2 a.m. text. Sure, it's probably worked out for someone in the long run, but for the rest of us? A flash in the pan that turns out to be fool's gold. Alas. At least you have this tasty drink.

1 Add the tequila, grapefruit juice, and lime juice to a highball glass filled with ice and stir.

2 Top with the grapefruit soda, stir again, and garnish with the grapefruit wheel.

INGREDIENTS

1¼ oz. tequila

2 oz. pineapple juice

1 oz. fresh lemon juice

¼ oz. grenadine

1 pineapple wedge (garnish)

1 maraschino cherry (garnish)

GLASSWARE

Rocks glass

"Why are you leaving the house?" "Why are you taking that road?" Better question—why did I think it was a good idea to let someone like that monitor my every movement? Turn off that location and find your happy place with this pineapple-forward treat.

1 Place the cocktail ingredients in a cocktail shaker filled with ice, shake vigorously, and strain into a rocks glass filled with ice.

2 Garnish with the pineapple wedge and maraschino cherry.

INGREDIENTS

Salt, for the rim

½ oz. lime juice

1 oz. tequila

½ oz. orange liqueur

1 oz. cranberry juice

1 lime wheel (garnish)

Handful of fresh cranberries (garnish)

GLASSWARE

Rocks glass

love bomb

There's a difference between a love bomb and a honeymoon stage, and those of us who have experienced the former can tell you—it kind of rocks in the short term until you figure out what's going on. Then it sucks. But hey, this cocktail will never turn on you—delicious every time!

1 Wet the rim of a rocks glass and dip it into salt.

2 Place the cocktail ingredients in a cocktail shaker filled with ice and shake vigorously.

3 Place ice in the rimmed glass, strain the cocktail into it, and garnish with the lime wheel and handful of cranberries.

INGREDIENTS

1¼ oz. tequila

¼ oz. Grand Marnier

1 lime (juiced)

1 oz. cranberry juice

1 orange slice (garnish)

GLASSWARE

Cocktail glass (chilled)

Sometimes you date someone who brands themselves as "blunt" or who has a "dark sense of humor." Unfortunately, sometimes those people just turn out to be plain mean. The things people do in the name of being honest!

1 Place the cocktail ingrecients in a cocktail shaker filled with ice and shake vigorously.

2 Strain into a chilled cocktail glass and garnish with the orange slice.

INGREDIENTS

Salt, for the rim

2 oz. silver tequila

¾ cup fresh honeydew melon, diced

4–5 mint leaves

2 oz. fresh lime juice

1 oz. orange liqueur

¾ cup ice

1 mint sprig (garnish)

GLASSWARE

Rocks glass

situationship

Almost everyone has been there. It's the worst kind of will-they-won't-they. Whether you're the one waiting for a text or the one trying to decide if this thing is worth the time and effort, it's nearly never as fun as it is anxiety-inducing. Soothe your nerves with this smooth libation.

1 Wet the rim of a rocks glass and dip it into salt.

2 Place the cocktail ingredients in a blender and puree until smooth.

3 Pour the cocktail into the glass and garnish with the mint sprig.

INGREDIENTS

1 oz. gold tequila

1 oz. ginger ale

2 oz. grapefruit juice

1 dash orange liqueur

1 grapefruit slice (garnish)

1 maraschino cherry (garnish)

GLASSWARE

Highball glass

hot and cold

One day you're crazy in love, and the next day your love is driving you crazy. It may sound like a fun roller coaster, but it's not. Exhilarating, yes, but so, so exhausting in the long run. Cool down with this fresh, fruity drink.

1 Add ice to a highball glass, then add the tequila, ginger ale, grapefruit juice, and orange liqueur.

2 Stir until thoroughly mixed.

3 Garnish with the grapefruit slice and maraschino cherry.

VARATION

If you don't have a grapefruit slice available, an orange slice will do.

INGREDIENTS

1 oz. tequila

½ oz. Midori

2 oz. sour mix

2 maraschino cherries (garnish)

GLASSWARE

Cocktail glass (chilled)

center of the universe

If you've ever gotten into a relationship only to find out that you were apparently dating the king of the world, this drink is for you. These divine beings walk amongst us mortals, occasionally deigning to date one of us and absolutely ruin our lives with their insufferable egos.

1 Place the cocktail ingredients in a cocktail shaker filled with crushed ice and shake until chilled.

2 Strain into a chilled cocktail glass and garnish with the maraschino cherries.

INGREDIENTS

Salt, for the rim

4 oz. reposado tequila

5-7 mint leaves

1 tablespoon cucumber, diced

2 oz. fresh lime juice

2 oz. mint syrup or agave nectar

Mint leaves (garnish)

1 lime wedge (garnish)

Cucumber slices (garnish)

GLASSWARE

Rocks glass

green-eyed monster

Look, it's normal to get a little jealous from time to time. But the people this cocktail is named after don't handle it quite so well. Drown that monster with this delightful refreshment.

1 Wet the rim of a rocks glass and dip it into salt.

2 Add the tequila, mint leaves, and diced cucumber to a cocktail shaker and muddle.

3 Add ice, the lime juice, and mint syrup or agave nectar and shake vigorously.

4 Fill the glass with ice, strain the cocktail into the glass, and garnish with additional mint, the lime wedge, and the cucumber slices.

INGREDIENTS

2 oz. silver tequila

1 oz. Midori

5 oz. white grapefruit juice

1 grapefruit slice (garnish)

GLASSWARE

Highball glass

the terrible texter

"How was your day?"
"Fine"
"Got any fun plans later?"
"No"
. . .
You deserve better than one-word responses. You deserve this tasty drink.

1 Place the cocktail ingredients in a cocktail shaker, fill it two-thirds of the way with ice, and shake until chilled.

2 Strain over ice into a highball glass and garnish with the slice of grapefruit.

INGREDIENTS

1 oz. añejo tequila

½ oz. simple syrup (see page 8)

2-3 dashes orange bitters

Lemon peel (garnish)

GLASSWARE

Rocks glass (chilled)

There's a common misconception that you have to be rich to attract a gold digger. Not so! Most everyone is a potential victim of a partner who simply does not believe that they should ever have to pay a penny or lift a finger. Your money is much better spent elsewhere—for instance, on procuring the ingredients for this crisp, warming drink.

1 Place the tequila, simple syrup, and bitters in a chilled rocks glass and stir.

2 Add 1 to 2 medium ice cubes to the glass, stir for 30 to 45 seconds, and garnish with the lemon peel.

INGREDIENTS

1½ oz. silver tequila

½ oz. sweet vermouth

½ oz. triple sec

1 splash grenadine

GLASSWARE

Cocktail glass

Even if someone is so nice, or generous, or good-looking, sometimes they're also just *so boring*. If you're on your third date and you find yourself thinking more about what you're doing afterward . . . you may need this drink to get through it.

1 Add the tequila, vermouth, triple sec, and grenadine to a cocktail shaker filled with ice.

2 Shake vigorously.

3 Strain the resulting mixture into a cocktail glass.

INGREDIENTS

Salt, for the rim

1½ oz. silver tequila

1½ oz. St-Germain Elderflower Liqueur

1⅓ oz. fresh lime juice

1 splash seltzer water, to top (optional)

Edible flowers (garnish)

1 lime wheel (garnish)

1 mint sprig (garnish)

GLASSWARE

Wineglass

sniff test

Good hygiene is essential, but we all have those moments—maybe you skipped a shower on a busy morning or relied on a mint to cover up that garlicky lunch. Usually, though, most of us manage to smell pleasant, or at least neutral. If only that were true for *everyone*. Luckily, this cocktail is here to rescue your senses with floral notes and fragrant hints of citrus, pear, and passion fruit.

1 Wet the rim of a wineglass and dip it into salt.

2 Place the tequila, St-Germain, and lime juice in a cocktail shaker, add ice, and shake until chilled.

3 Fill the glass with ice, strain the cocktail into the glass, top with the seltzer (if desired), and garnish with the edible flowers, lime wheel, and mint sprig.

INGREDIENTS

Bee pollen, for the rim

Salt, for the rim

2½ oz. añejo tequila

2½ oz. honey syrup

½ oz. orange liqueur

1 oz. fresh lime juice

1 rosemary sprig (garnish)

GLASSWARE

Rocks glass

it didn't mean anything

If you've heard this line, we're very sorry. It's a wonder that this is such a standard excuse for cheating, because really, has this ever made anyone feel better? Baffling. But you know what might actually make you feel better? This beautiful golden-orange cocktail!

1 Wet the rim of a rocks glass and dip it into bee pollen and salt.

2 Place the cocktail ingredients in a cocktail shaker filled with ice and shake until chilled.

3 Strain the cocktail into the glass with ice and garnish with the rosemary sprig.

INGREDIENTS

1 oz. silver tequila

1 oz. blackberry liqueur

1 lime (juiced)

2 oz. ginger beer

Handful of blackberries (garnish)

1 mint sprig (garnish)

GLASSWARE

Highball glass

This one goes out to those of us who have goals, ambitions, and things we want out of life—and ex-partners that seemed to have no goal other than to make achieving *your* goals harder. You deserve someone who works as hard as you do to make the life of your dreams. Reward yourself for your efforts with this sweet-and-sour sipper.

1 Add the tequila, blackberry liqueur, and lime juice to a cocktail shaker filled with ice. Shake well.

2 Strain the resulting mixture into a highball glass filled with ice. Top with the ginger beer.

3 Garnish with the handful of blackberries and a mint sprig.

INGREDIENTS

Cocoa powder, for the rim

2 oz. tequila

1 oz. heavy cream

1 oz. crème de cacao

1 teaspoon Chambord

Chocolate shavings (garnish)

GLASSWARE

Cocktail glass (chilled)

If you're old enough to be reading this book, you're old enough to pick up the clothes off the floor and wipe down the sink. If you did all the cleaning in your last relationship, this drink is your chance to take a well-earned breather.

1 Wet the rim of a cocktail glass and dip it into cocoa powder.

2 Place the liquid ingredients in a cocktail shaker filled with ice, shake vigorously, and strain into a chilled cocktail glass.

3 Garnish with the chocolate shavings.

Trauma Dump, page 50

MEZCAL-ING ME DRUNK

Mezcal is tequila's dark, smoky cousin—the one who leaves a trail of mystery and sends "we need to talk" texts after midnight. Its flavor is as deep and layered as the riddles you tried to solve with that enigmatic ex. This chapter leans into mezcal's complexities, from earthy notes to smoldering tones, offering cocktails that remind you of when "smoke and mirrors" was a little too literal. Perfect for sipping as you toast the ones who dialed your number after a few, only to ghost you sober.

INGREDIENTS

1 oz. Del Maguey Chichicapa Mezcal

1 oz. Tequila Cabeza

½ oz. Amaro Averna

¼ oz. Royal Combier

3 mists of Angostura Bitters

1 torched strip of orange peel (garnish)

GLASSWARE

Wineglass

critical darling

There are scenarios in which constructive criticism is a positive thing. To a point. Some people take this way too far and make it their life's mission to pick apart every little thing you do. That's no way to live! If you've been the target of one such critic, you need this drink.

1 Place the mezcal, tequila, amaro, and Royal Combier in a wineglass and swirl.

2 Hold the strip of orange peel about 2 inches above a lit match for a couple of seconds. Twist and squeeze the peel over the lit match, while holding it above the cocktail and taking care to avoid the flames.

3 Mist the inside of the glass above the cocktail with the bitters and garnish with the torched strip of orange peel.

INGREDIENTS

1½ oz. reposado tequila

½ oz. mezcal

2 dashes Angostura Bitters

1 barspoon agave nectar

1 torched strip of orange peel (garnish)

GLASSWARE

Rocks glass

gaslighter

If you've ever had a partner who made you feel crazy, this cocktail is for you. Once you start questioning your reality around someone, it's a pretty clear sign that their toxicity is not worth whatever else you're getting out of the relationship. Burn it all down with this fiery masterpiece.

1 Place a large ice cube in a rocks glass. Add all of the cocktail ingredients and stir until chilled.

2 Hold the strip of orange peel about 2 inches above a lit match for a couple of seconds. Twist and squeeze the peel over the lit match, while holding it above the cocktail and taking care to avoid the flames.

3 Rub the torched peel around the rim of the glass, drop it into the drink, and enjoy.

INGREDIENTS

1 oz. mezcal

1 oz. silver tequila

1 oz. fresh lime juice

1 oz. pineapple juice

½ oz. agave nectar

1 mint sprig (garnish)

GLASSWARE

Coupe

Arguably the most important skill in a relationship is the ability to listen. But if you find yourself listening . . . and listening . . . and listening . . . day after day to a story that has seemingly no end, it may be time to find someone who will listen to you for a change. Perhaps you could have an actual conversation over a delicious drink like this one.

1 Place the cocktail ingredients in a cocktail shaker filled halfway with ice and shake vigorously.

2 Double-strain into a coupe and garnish with the mint sprig.

INGREDIENTS

1 oz. mezcal

1 oz. grapefruit juice

2 rosemary sprigs

2 oz. grapefruit soda

1 grapefruit slice (garnish)

GLASSWARE

Rocks glass

was that today?

Birthdays, anniversaries, important gatherings and events—you'd think these special occasions would be unforgettable, but some people simply do not care enough to remember the things that are important to you. Who needs them? Celebrate on your own with this fizzy refresher.

1 Add the mezcal, grapefruit juice, and 1 rosemary sprig to a cocktail shaker filled with ice. Shake well.

2 Strain the resulting mixture into a rocks glass filled with ice.

3 Top with the grapefruit soda and garnish with the grapefruit slice and the remaining rosemary sprig.

INGREDIENTS

Salt, for the rim

2 oz. silver tequila

1 oz. mezcal

1 oz. fresh lime juice

1 oz. simple syrup (see page 8)

4-5 blackberries

1 lime slice (garnish)

Several blackberries (garnish)

1 mint sprig (garnish)

1 splash seltzer water (optional)

GLASSWARE

Rocks glass

trauma dump

Picture this: You're fifteen minutes into a first date with someone you've never met before. At this point, what you probably should know is their name, what they enjoy, maybe what they do for work. But instead, you know exactly what their parents did to them to make them to kind of person that would tell you their darkest secret immediately upon meeting. And now we all need therapy. In the meantime, maybe this mysterious take on the classic Margarita will help you out.

1 Wet the rim of a rocks glass and dip it into salt.

2 Place the cocktail ingredients in a cocktail shaker, muddle, fill with ice, and shake vigorously.

3 Fill the glass with ice, strain the cocktail into the glass, garnish with the lime slice, blackberries, and mint sprig, and top with the splash of seltzer, if desired.

INGREDIENTS

Salt, for the rim

1½ oz. resposado tequila

½ oz. mezcal

¾ oz. Amaro Nonino Quintessentia

¾ oz. fresh lime juice

½ oz. agave nectar

1 lime wheel (garnish)

GLASSWARE

Margarita glass

All relationships have their ups and downs. What we all hope for is someone who will stay with us, even when we're not at our best. But not everyone has the stomach for the journey. This cocktail is dedicated to those who stayed the course while their partners jumped ship the first time they saw a wave coming. Ah, let the sharks have them.

1 Wet the rim of a margarita glass and dip it into salt.

2 Place the cocktail ingredients in a cocktail shaker filled with ice and shake until it is very cold.

3 Double-strain into a margarita glass or a coupe and garnish with the lime wheel.

INGREDIENTS

1¼ oz. mezcal

1⅔ oz. pear juice

⅓ oz. simple syrup (see page 8)

Champagne, to top

1 pear slice (garnish)

GLASSWARE

Champagne flute

It's fun to dress up, and it's exciting to own nice things. But if you've ever met someone who can't go without them for even a moment, it can be very hard to keep up with their expectations. Take care of yourself first with this bubbly treat.

1. Fill a shaker with ice, the mezcal, pear juice, and simple syrup.
2. Shake 4 or 5 times to aerate the cocktail.
3. Pour it into a champagne flute and top with champagne.
4. Garnish with the pear slice.

INGREDIENTS

2 tablespoons green apple juice

2 tablespoons tangerine juice

2 tablespoons pineapple juice

2 tablespoons blueberry juice

2 tablespoons pink grapefruit juice

2 tablespoons blood orange juice

1⅔ oz. mezcal, such as Alipús Santa Ana

3⅓ oz. tonic water

Several pieces of rainbow-striped candy (garnish)

GLASSWARE

Highball glass (chilled)

compensating

Some people show up with flowers, others with love bombs and extravagant promises. Much like that ex who traded personal growth for grand gestures, this cocktail is both excessive and oddly satisfying. It is a sipping drink; the more the fruit ice cubes melt, the fruitier the cocktail will get. But be warned: This cocktail must be made ahead of time, so it would probably be best to make it when you're able to prepare the ice cubes the night prior.

1 Pour each juice in its own spot of an ice cube tray and place the tray in the freezer overnight or until frozen.

2 In a chilled highball glass, arrange the ice cubes according to the rainbow spectrum colors (if you can), and then pour the mezcal over them.

3 Top with the tonic water and garnish with the rainbow-striped candy.

INGREDIENTS

1 oz. mezcal

1 oz. Aperol

⅔ oz. fraise liqueur (strawberry liqueur)

1 strawberry slice (garnish)

GLASSWARE

Rocks glass (chilled)

Being a musician, artist, or creative isn't an inherently bad thing. But if you've ever dated someone who was seriously considering quitting their day job to pursue a passion they didn't have the skills or talent to back up . . . woof. Once you stop cringing at the memory, do your best to move on with the help of this sweet alternative to the classic Negroni.

1 Fill a mixing glass with ice.

2 Pour the mezcal, Aperol, and fraise liqueur into the chilled mixing glass, and stir rapidly with a barspoon for 17 to 20 seconds.

3 Strain into a chilled rocks glass over a block of ice.

4 Garnish with the strawberry slice.

INGREDIENTS

1⅔ oz. mezcal

4 tablespoons coconut sorbet

⅚ oz. pineapple juice

⅔ oz. freshly squeezed lime juice

½ oz. simple syrup (see page 8)

3 pineapple leaves (garnish)

1 Luxardo maraschino cherry (garnish)

1 lime wedge (garnish)

GLASSWARE

Highball glass (chilled)

touch grass

Just fifty years ago, we wouldn't have had to deal with this. But nowadays it's so easy to get sucked into endless screen time, and some people just can't be torn away. Too bad for them—you'll be here in reality sipping this tropical dream of a drink.

1 Combine the mezcal, coconut sorbet, pineapple juice, lime juice, and simple syrup in a cocktail shaker.

2 Fill with ice cubes to the top and close the shaker. Hard shake for 10 seconds, until the shaker is frozen.

3 Fill a chilled highball glass with ice and double-strain the cocktail into it.

4 Garnish with the pineapple leaves, Luxardo maraschino cherry, and lime wedge.

Spoken For, page 84

DRIVING ME VODKA-RAZY

Ah, vodka. Crystal clear, endlessly adaptable, but oh-so-deadly when underestimated. Vodka reminds us of those exes who seemed uncomplicated at first but managed to drive us absolutely bananas once we got to know them. This chapter is a tribute to the clean slates that somehow left devastating chaos in their wake. With every sleek, dangerously smooth cocktail, you'll revisit those whirlwind romances that felt perfect until they didn't—but at least vodka, unlike those exes, never hides who it is.

INGREDIENTS

3 oz. vodka

1 oz. DeKuyper Pucker Sour Apple Schnapps Liqueur

1 oz. triple sec

2 thin slices of apple (garnish)

GLASSWARE

Cocktail glass

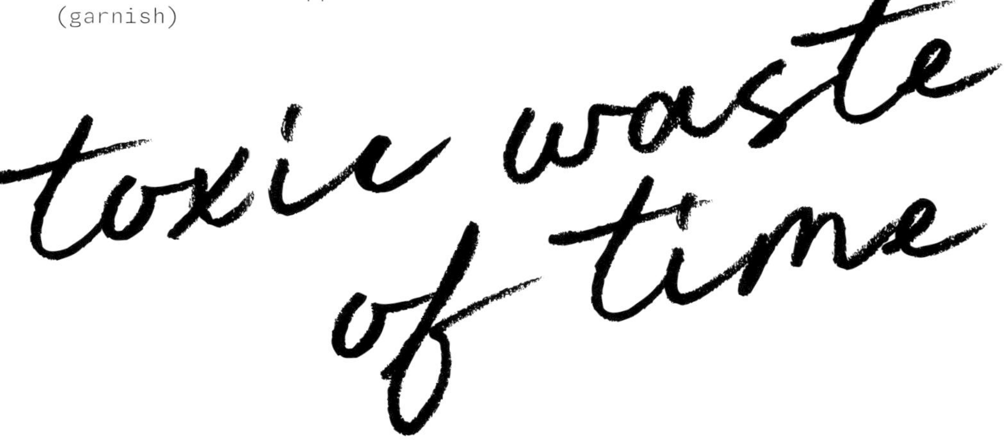

Some people are just bad for you. They might be bad people, or they might just be a terrible match for you specifically. Either way, their toxicity creeps into your relationship and your life, slowly poisoning everything you thought was good. This sour apple concoction may not be the antidote, but it's worth a try!

1 Add the vodka, Sour Apple Schnapps Liqueur, and triple sec to a cocktail shaker filled with ice and shake vigorously.

2 Strain the resulting mixture into a cocktail glass.

3 Garnish with the thin slices of apple.

INGREDIENTS

1 handful of blueberries

1 handful of raspberries

1 oz. raspberry vodka

2 oz. club soda

1 splash grenadine

1 mint sprig (garnish)

GLASSWARE

Highball glass

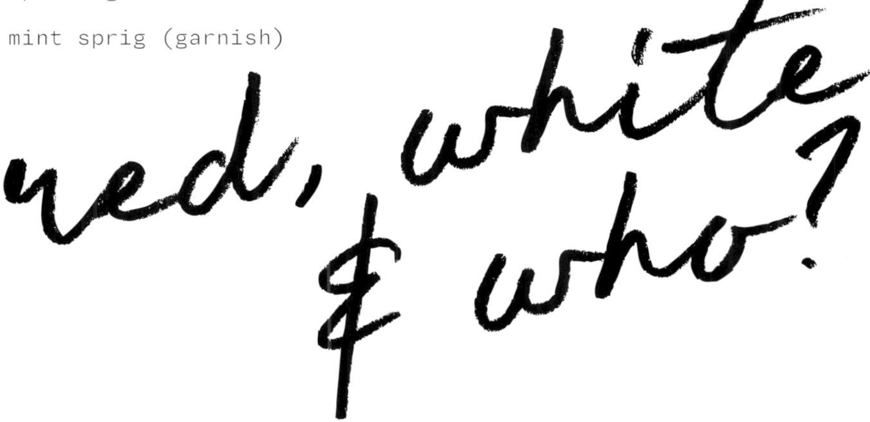

Can't we all get along? Well . . . maybe not always. Politics are a notoriously tricky topic, and disagreements on the subject have caused the downfall of many a relationship. Sometimes you realize you'll just never see eye to eye. When that happens, you can always turn to this sweet, delicious knockoff sangria—all the flavor without the hassle.

1 Add the blueberries and raspberries to a highball glass, and then fill the glass with ice.

2 Add the raspberry vodka and club soda.

3 Top with the splash of grenadine, adding more if needed to achieve the desired color. Garnish with the mint sprig.

INGREDIENTS

2 drops of dry vermouth

1¾ oz. vodka

Olives, skewered (garnish)

GLASSWARE

Cocktail glass (chilled)

Manners may not be as cut-and-dried as they once were, but a modicum of decorum is still expected in most circles. Whether they were raised in a barn or just want to rebel against social standards, some people take pride in being inconsiderate and rude. If you've ever had the misfortune of dating one of these people, this drink is for you.

1 Place the vermouth in a cocktail shaker filled with ice and add the vodka. Stir or shake.

2 Strain into a chilled cocktail glass and garnish with skewered olives.

INGREDIENTS

2 oz. vodka

½ oz. dry vermouth

1 splash pickle juice

1 to 2 cornichons, skewered (garnish)

GLASSWARE

Cocktail glass

What is there to say? The ick is an undefinable but unescapable phenomenon, and if you've experienced it, then you understand. The strongest among us may be able to move past an ick, but for most of us . . . well, you can drink this to try to forget.

1 Place the vodka, vermouth, and pickle juice in a mixing glass filled with ice. Stir until thoroughly combined.

2 Strain the resulting mixture into a cocktail glass.

3 Garnish with 1 to 2 cornichons, skewered on a toothpick.

INGREDIENTS

1 oz. vodka

2 oz. cherry vcdka

1 oz. lime juice

1 dash grenadine

1 lime twist (garnish)

2 maraschino cherries (garnish)

GLASSWARE

Cocktail glass

Sometimes you see a red flag and ignore it . . . and then another . . . and then another . . . until you have a bouquet of red flags. At this rate, who needs roses? If you spotted a red flag and immediately dipped, you are who we all aspire to be. And if you collected the bouquet . . . we get it. You'll do better next time!

1 Add the vodka, cherry vodka, lime juice, and grenadine to a cocktail shaker filled with ice. Shake vigorously.

2 Strain the resulting mixture into a cocktail glass.

3 Garnish with the lime twist and maraschino cherries.

INGREDIENTS

1 oz. strawberry vodka

1 oz. vanilla vodka

2 oz. cream (to top)

1 splash grenadine

1 fresh strawberry (garnish)

GLASSWARE

Rocks glass

time after time

Do you ever feel like you're living on a loop, having the same argument over and over again? Having the same argument over and over again? Having the same argument over and over again? Break out of the cycle with this colorful cocktail.

1 Pour the strawberry vodka and vanilla vodka over ice in a rocks glass. Top with the cream and stir until thoroughly mixed.

2 Finish with the splash of grenadine for color. Garnish with the fresh strawberry.

INGREDIENTS

Salt (for the rim)

2 oz. vodka

2¼ oz. fresh grapefruit juice

½ oz. Giffard Crème de Pamplemousse Rose

1 spoonful of Luxardo liqueur

1 grapefruit slice (garnish)

1 mint sprig (garnish)

GLASSWARE

Highball glass

If you're someone who knows what they want, good for you. If you're someone who doesn't know what they want, maybe try to figure that out before leading anyone on for years and years with no intention of ever actually committing. Just an idea!

1 Wet the rim of a highball glass and then dip it into salt.

2 Fill the glass with ice, and then add all of the remaining ingredients, except for the garnishes. Stir until combined.

3 Garnish with the grapefruit slice and mint sprig.

INGREDIENTS

1 oz. Deep Eddy Ruby Red Grapefruit Vodka

4 oz. lemonade

Shiner Ruby Redbird beer (to top)

1 lemon wheel (garnish)

GLASSWARE

Pint glass

There's nothing wrong with letting loose once in a while. But if you found yourself constantly having to tuck your passed-out partner into bed after a few too many . . . you deserve to be the one to let loose for a change.

1 Layer the grapefruit vodka, lemonade, and beer in a pint glass.

2 Garnish with the lemon wheel.

INGREDIENTS

1 oz. raspberry vodka

1 splash triple sec

2 oz. lemonade

1 splash grenadine

1 lemon slice (garnish)

GLASSWARE

Highball glass

Love me, love me not . . . who knows? With some people, it would be easier to figure out the meaning of life than the meaning of their words. When you need a break from that headache, this refreshing glass of fruit flavors has your back.

1 Add ice to a highball glass, and then add the raspberry vodka and triple sec.

2 Fill the rest of the glass with the lemonade and top with the splash of grenadine to add an inviting red hue to the drink.

3 Garnish with the lemon slice.

INGREDIENTS

1 oz. cranberry vodka

2 oz. lemonade

1 splash lime juice

GLASSWARE

Cocktail glass

Apologizing is hard. Making a genuine apology is even harder. But if you can't ever own up to your actions or you think "I'm sorry you feel that way" counts . . . you're the reason this cocktail was created.

1 Fill a cocktail shaker with ice and add the cranberry vodka, lemonade, and lime juice. Shake well.

2 Strain the resulting mixture into a cocktail glass.

INGREDIENTS

1 oz. vanilla vodka

1 pinch brown sugar

3 oz. apple cider

Dusting of cinramon (garnish)

1 cinnamon stick (garnish)

1 star anise (garnish)

GLASSWARE

Mason jar or glass mug

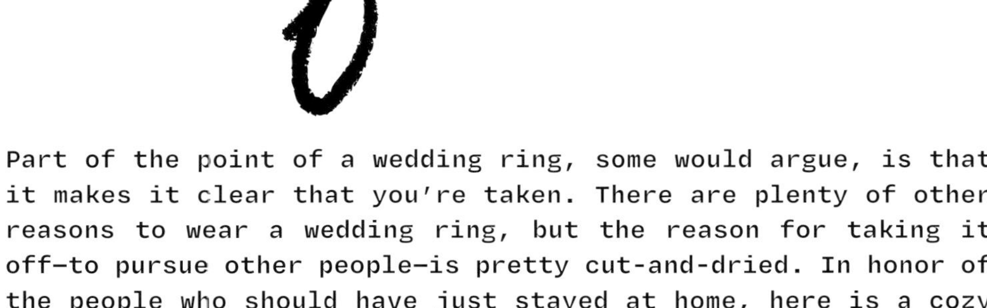

Part of the point of a wedding ring, some would argue, is that it makes it clear that you're taken. There are plenty of other reasons to wear a wedding ring, but the reason for taking it off—to pursue other people—is pretty cut-and-dried. In honor of the people who should have just stayed at home, here is a cozy drink that captures all the best flavors of homemade apple pie.

1 Add the vanilla vodka and brown sugar to a mason jar or glass mug and stir them together.

2 Pour the apple cider over the top and garnish with the dusting of cinnamon, the cinnamon stick, and the star anise.

INGREDIENTS

1½ oz. vodka

½ oz. fresh lime juice

1 lime wheel (garnish)

GLASSWARE

Cocktail glass

Sometimes you'll be having a great conversation, and then the person you're talking to just stops responding. And then you never hear from them again. Sometimes you'll even get ghosted mid-relationship. Sometimes you'll even get ghosted in the middle of—

1 Place the vodka and fresh lime juice in a mixing glass filled with ice and strain into a cocktail glass.

2 Garnish with the lime wheel.

INGREDIENTS

2 oz. vodka

1 oz. blueberry liqueur

1 oz. lemon juice

1 small handful of blueberries (garnish)

1 lemon wedge (garnish)

1 mint sprig (garnish)

GLASSWARE

Rocks glass

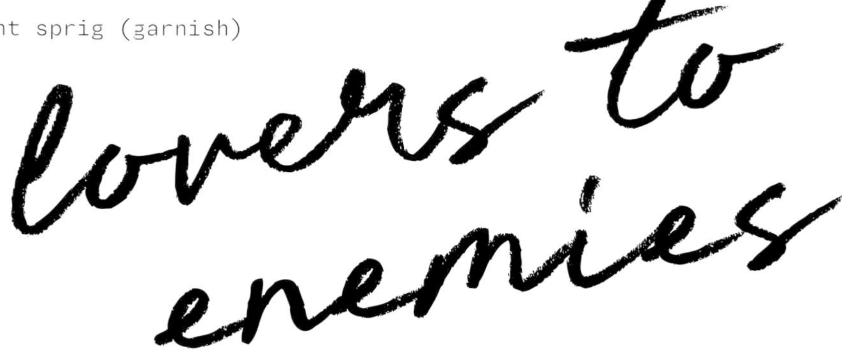

I know, I know . . . the trope is "enemies to lovers." But "lovers to enemies" probably happens a lot more in the real world. This drink starts off with the sweetness of blueberry liqueur and then reveals the tartness of the lemon underneath. Sound familiar?

1 Add the vodka, blueberry liqueur, and lemon juice to a cocktail shaker filled with ice. Shake well.

2 Strain the resulting mixture into a rocks glass. Add the desired amount of ice.

3 Garnish with the small handful of blueberries, the lemon wedge, and the mint sprig.

INGREDIENTS

3 oz. vodka

1 oz. Kahlúa

2 oz. espresso

1 handful of espresso beans (garnish)

GLASSWARE

Coupe

Having friends at work is normal. Having a spouse at work? Now that's crazy. Who even thought of this? And if you've ever had a partner get together with their supposedly platonic work spouse, you'll agree.

1 Add the vodka, Kahlúa, and espresso to a cocktail shaker filled with ice. Shake vigorously

2 Strain the resulting mixture into a coupe.

3 Garnish with the espresso beans.

INGREDIENTS

Colorful sprinkles (for the rim)

2 oz. vanilla vodka

2 oz. heavy cream

1 oz. white chocolate liqueur

1 splash amaretto

GLASSWARE

Cocktail glass

There's nothing like getting a little wild at a great party. But all great parties end. And if you've dated someone who does not know when to quit, then you're probably exhausted just thinking about it. Relax with this fun treat.

1 Wet the rim of a cocktail glass and press it into colorful sprinkles.

2 Combine the liquid ingredients in a cocktail shaker filled with ice. Shake well.

3 Strain the resulting mixture into the cocktail glass.

INGREDIENTS

2 oz. vodka

GLASSWARE

Shot glass

This is a shot of vodka.

1 Pour the vodka.

2 Drink it.

Switched Teams, page 102

RUM FOR YOUR LIFE

From tropical beaches to dark and stormy nights, rum has always been the spirit of adventure and escape. This chapter is for the exes who left you feeling both swept away and completely shipwrecked. Sweet, spiced, or delightfully over the top, these drinks are your ticket to running far, far away from the chaos—and toward better adventures.

INGREDIENTS

2 oz. light rum

1 oz. triple sec

1 oz. lime juice

Frozen watermelon (approx. 1 cup per oz of rum)

Watermelon wedge (garnish)

GLASSWARE

Rocks glass

Not every relationship ends in fiery disaster. Some relationships end just because you realize you're not done dating yet. You want to meet new people and explore what the world has to offer. And there's nothing wrong with that! Cheers to your next adventure!

1 Add the rum, triple sec, lime juice, and frozen watermelon to a blender and blend until smooth.

2 Serve in rocks glasses and garnish with watermelon wedges.

3 Pour leftover mixture into a freezer bag and freeze for later. (NOTE: Freeze before the mixture has time to thaw.)

4 Return to the freezer for a still-frozen cocktail whenever the mood strikes.

INGREDIENTS

6 mint leaves

½ lime (juiced)

1 oz. white rum

2 oz. cola

1 lime wedge (garnish)

1 mint sprig (garnish)

GLASSWARE

Highball glass

The name of this cocktail lends itself to two uniquely terrible things a partner can do. One: they air out your dirty laundry for the world to see. Maybe they can't keep a secret from their friends or their family, and your private business becomes not so private. Two: they literally just never do their laundry. Gross.

1 Tear the mint leaves in half and add them to the bottom of the highball glass. Add the lime juice and muddle together.

2 Add ice to the glass and pour in the rum and cola. Stir until thoroughly mixed.

3 Garnish with the lime wedge and mint sprig.

INGREDIENTS

Sugar, for the rim

2 oz. white rum

1 oz. lime juice

1 oz. triple sec

1 splash simple syrup (see page 8)

1 lime wheel (garnish)

GLASSWARE

Cocktail glass

switched teams

Sometimes self-discovery takes a while! It would be nice if that revelation didn't come in the midst of a loving relationship with you, but hey, things happen. If you've dated someone until they realized you're not quite their type, then this twist on the classic Daiquiri is for you.

1 Wet the rim of a cocktail glass and press it into sugar.

2 Fill a cocktail shaker with ice and add the liquid ingredients. Shake well. Strain the contents of the cocktail shaker into the cocktail glass.

3 Garnish with the lime wheel.

VARIATION

Everyone on earth has heard of the Strawberry Daiquiri, and you can make one by adding a bit of strawberry schnapps in place of the triple sec. If you want the frozen version of the drink, add about half a cup of ice and blend it all together.

INGREDIENTS

1 oz. light rum

1 oz. coconut rum

1 oz. melon liqueur

3 oz. pineapple juice

1 maraschino cherry (garnish)

GLASSWARE

Rocks glass

big yikes

Unlike the Ick (page 71), which is often subtle and occasionally difficult to explain, the Big Yikes is undeniable. It is so cringeworthy and embarrassing that no sane person would stay afterward. What is it exactly? Well, you'll know it when you see it.

1 Add the liquid ingredients to a cocktail shaker filled with ice. Shake well.

2 Strain the resulting mixture into a rocks glass filled with ice.

3 Garnish with the maraschino cherry.

INGREDIENTS

1 banana

1 oz. vanilla rum

1 oz. banana rum

1 oz. cream

1 dusting nutmeg (garnish)

1 banana slice (garnish)

GLASSWARE

Highball glass

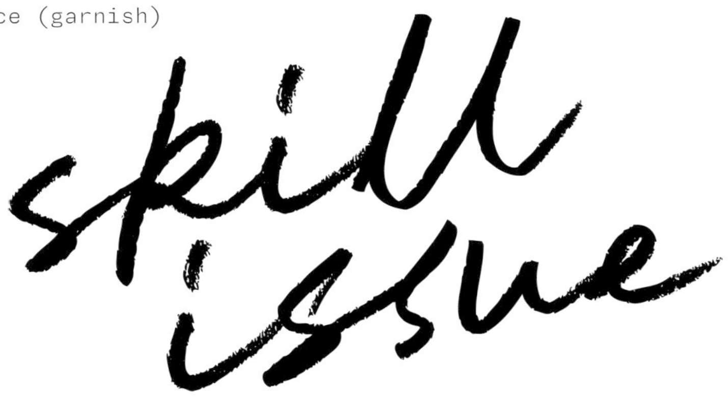

There are many, many things that make up a healthy relationship. And if someone is really lacking in, ahem, certain areas, that can be tough to get past. Yes, all skills are learnable, but sometimes the puzzle pieces just don't fit right. And if you've been there, this concoction is all you.

1 Cut one slice off the banana and reserve for a garnish.

2 Put the rest of the banana, vanilla rum, banana rum, and cream in a blender and blend until smooth.

3 Pour the resulting mixture into a highball glass and dust with a bit of nutmeg. Garnish with the banana slice.

INGREDIENTS

6 mint leaves

3 jalapeño slices

1 oz. white rum

2 oz. lime seltzer

1 splash simple syrup (see page 8)

1 mint sprig (garnish)

1 cucumber slice (garnish)

GLASSWARE

Highball glass

wandering eye

Even if your partner doesn't have wandering hands, a wandering eye can be unbelievably frustrating. You've got plenty for them to focus on, so what is the deal? Well, it's got nothing to do with you. Focus on yourself with this spicy take on a simplified Mojito recipe.

1 Muddle the mint leaves and jalapeño slices with the simple syrup in the bottom of a highball glass, then add ice.

2 Add the rum and seltzer and stir until thoroughly mixed.

3 Garnish with the mint sprig and cucumber slice.

NOTE: If this drink is too spicy for you, try removing the seeds from the jalapeño slices before muddling. Most of the heat from the peppers is in the seeds, and you may find that removing them leaves you with the perfect spice level for your palate.

INGREDIENTS

1 oz. dark rum

1 oz. coffee liqueur

1 oz. chocolate liqueur

3 oz. heavy cream

Whipped cream (garnish)

Chocolate sauce (garnish)

GLASSWARE

Rocks glass

A good relationship with your mother is an amazing gift. But a codependent relationship with your mother . . . that's another story. In most relationships, there's only enough room for two people. When a third person constantly inserts themselves, it's no wonder there's no space for you. But they deserve each other–and you deserve this milkshake-adjacent cocktail.

1 Add the rum, coffee liqueur, and chocolate liqueur to a cocktail shaker filled with ice. Shake well.

2 Strain the resulting mixture into a rocks glass filled with ice. Top with heavy cream.

3 Garnish with a dollop of whipped cream and a drizzle of chocolate sauce if desired.

INGREDIENTS

1 oz. dark rum

2 oz. ginger beer

½ lime (juiced)

1 splash orgeat syrup

1 lime wedge (garnish)

GLASSWARE

Highball glass

Dating is such a pain, so when you find someone you get along really well with, it's natural to get your hopes up. And nearly nothing is worse than realizing that you're the rebound. Either they're not over their ex, or they're *really* not over them and they'll be getting back together next week. Here is a delicious consolation prize.

1 Add ice to a highball glass and pour in the rum, ginger beer, and lime juice. Stir until thoroughly mixed.

2 Finish with a splash of orgeat syrup. Do not stir.

3 Garnish with the lime wedge.

INGREDIENTS

20 mint leaves

4 lime wedges (juiced)

1 oz. white rum

2 oz. lemonade

4 lemon wheels (garnish)

GLASSWARE

Highball glass

weaponized incompetence

"You should just do the dishes. You're so much better at it, and I'm hopeless with this stuff." ***So learn!*** **When someone pretends to be incompetent just to make your life harder, it's time to go. Vent to your friends and share this delicious punch. This recipe makes four servings.**

1 Tear the mint leaves in half and add them to a pitcher. Juice the lime wedges into the pitcher and muddle the ingredients together as best you can.

2 Add ice, rum, and lemonade. Stir until thoroughly mixed.

3 Pour into individual glasses and garnish with lemon wheels.

INGREDIENTS

1 oz. spiced rum

2 oz. cola

1 scoop vanilla ice cream

GLASSWARE

Pint glass

permanently in between jobs

Jobs come and go, but drive and ambition are pretty constant. If you find someone who doesn't have a job, that's not always a red flag—stuff happens. But if you meet someone with no desire to *ever* get a job . . . run.

1 Pour the spiced rum and cola into a pint glass.

2 Add a scoop of vanilla ice cream, and serve with a long spoon.

INGREDIENTS

1 oz. white rum

1 oz. triple sec

2 oz. club soda

1 splash grenadine

1 maraschino cherry (garnish)

GLASSWARE

Rocks glass

wambulance

Everyone loves a little gossip or a good vent session, but some people take things way too far. There's a difference between needing to decompress occasionally and just being a negative person. If someone is constantly whining, then all you can do is mix yourself up a Wambulance.

1 Fill a rocks glass with ice, then add the white rum and triple sec. Top with club soda.

2 Finish with a splash of grenadine. Garnish with the maraschino cherry.

INGREDIENTS

1 oz. dark rum

1 oz. pineapple juice

1 oz. orange juice

2 drops bitters

1 pineapple wedge (garnish)

3 pineapple leaves (garnish)

GLASSWARE

Rocks glass

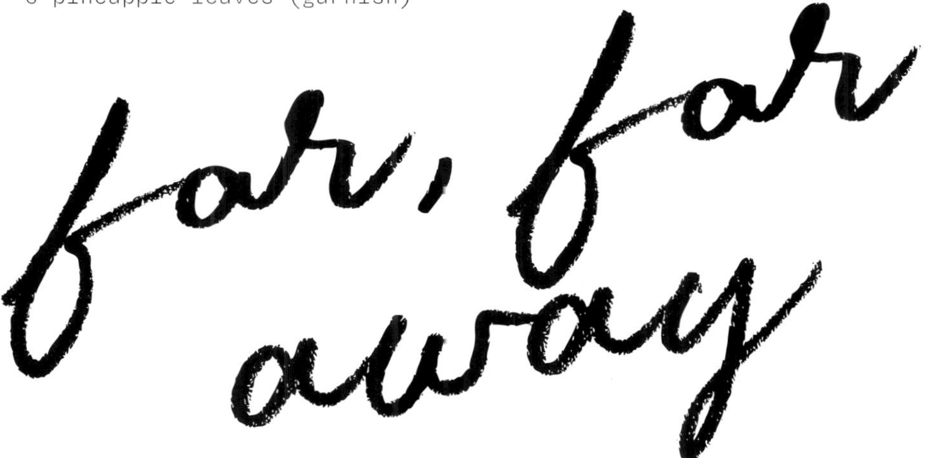

Absence makes the heart grow fonder ... until it breaks your heart entirely. Even in the modern age, navigating a long-distance relationship is tricky. When you need something to soothe the ache, try this island-inspired punch.

1 Add the rum, juices, and bitters to a cocktail shaker filled with ice. Shake well.

2 Strain the resulting mixture into a rocks glass filled with ice.

3 Garnish with the wedge of pireapple and 3 pineapple leaves.

INGREDIENTS

1 squeeze lemon juice

3 mint leaves (or 1 dash crème de menthe)

1 oz. rum

2 oz. seltzer (any flavor)

1 or 2 mint sprigs (garnish)

GLASSWARE

Highball glass

Being with another person changes you. It's pretty hard not to find yourself growing together, for better or for worse. The ability to change and adapt is an admirable quality—just not one that everyone has, unfortunately. If you've ever dated someone who was physically incapable of change or compromise, this drink is for you.

1 Muddle the mint and lemon juice in the bottom of a highball glass.

2 Add the rum and seltzer.

3 Fill glass with ice and stir thoroughly. Garnish with mint sprigs.

INGREDIENTS

1 oz. rum

1 oz. Crown Royal Whisky

1 oz. brandy

1 splash grenadine

1 maraschino cherry (garnish)

GLASSWARE

Rocks glass

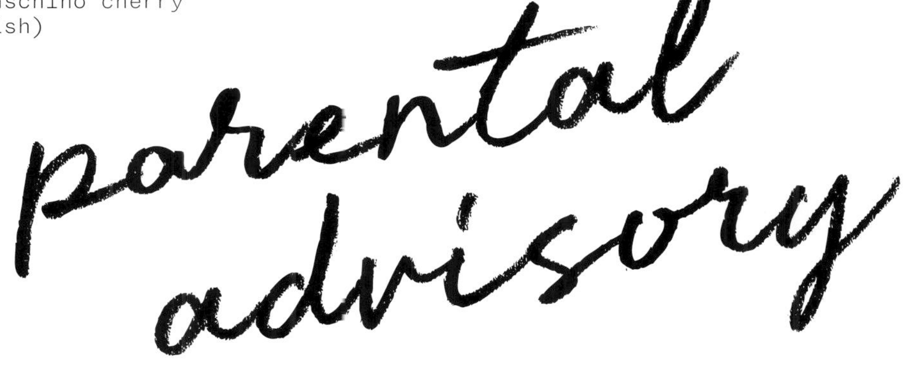

Meeting the parents is a terrifying but usually necessary step in a serious relationship. While it's normal for it to be a little awkward and for it to take time to build rapport, sometimes things just go sideways. Relationships can survive the parents hating the partner, but it ain't easy at the best of times. And when the worst of times comes around, this boozy concoction featuring three different types of alcohol is here for you.

1 Add the rum, whiskey, brandy and grenadine to a cocktail shaker filled with ice.

2 Shake well.

3 Strain the resulting mixture into a rocks glass filled with ice.

4 Garnish with a maraschino cherry.

INGREDIENTS

1 oz. maple syrup

2 oz. Irish cream liqueur

1 oz. rum

1 oz. milk or cream

GLASSWARE

Cocktail glass

There's having a routine, and there's being stuck in a rut. Who doesn't want a few exciting new things in their life from time to time, even if it's something small and simple? And if that turns out to be impossible with your partner in the picture, this comforting cocktail is something new and fun for you to try.

1 Add the maple syrup, Irish cream liqueur, rum, and milk or cream to a cocktail shaker filled with ice.

2 Shake vigorously.

3 Strain the resulting mixture into a cocktail glass.

Double Text, page 136

PUR-GIN YOU FROM MY LIFE

Gin is the ex who always had a sharp wit, impeccable taste, and a knack for getting under your skin—in the best and worst ways. With a botanical bite and a nose for drama, gin doesn't just show up; it announces itself. From crisp and classic to bold and bitter, these cocktails cut through the noise and leave a lingering impression—just like the ex you're still trying to forget (but kind of want to text).

INGREDIENTS

2 oz. gin

1 oz. triple sec

1 splash lemon juice

1 splash maple syrup

1 lemon twist (garnish)

GLASSWARE

Cocktail glass

Just about everyone wants a partner who adores them. When you find a person who wants to spend all their time with you, it's a wonderful gift. But if the honeymoon phase ends and they still want to spend every single second with you, that kind of clinginess can become suffocating. Reclaim your own time with this breakfast-inspired martini.

1 Pour the liquid ingredients into a cocktail shaker with ice and shake well to completely integrate the maple syrup.

2 Strain the resulting mixture into a cocktail glass. Garnish with the lemon twist.

INGREDIENTS

1 oz. gin

1 oz. Campari

½ oz. sweet vermouth

1 orange twist (garnish)

GLASSWARE

Rocks glass

brutally bittersweet

While the majority of the recipes in this book are inspired by breakups with partners who just completely blew it, this one is dedicated to the endings that broke your heart for another reason. If the stars just didn't align despite the love you had for each other, it can be difficult to savor the sweet parts amidst the bitter situation. This cocktail, inspired by the classic Negroni, uses sweet vermouth and the floral notes of Campari to help you celebrate the good with the bad.

1 Add the gin, Campari, and sweet vermouth to a cocktail shaker filled with ice. Shake well.

2 Strain the resulting mixture into a rocks glass filled with ice.

3 Garnish with the twist of orange.

INGREDIENTS

2 oz. gin

1 oz. blueberry simple syrup

½ lemon (juiced)

1 oz. club soda

1 lemon wheel (garnish)

Blueberries (garnish)

GLASSWARE

Rocks glass

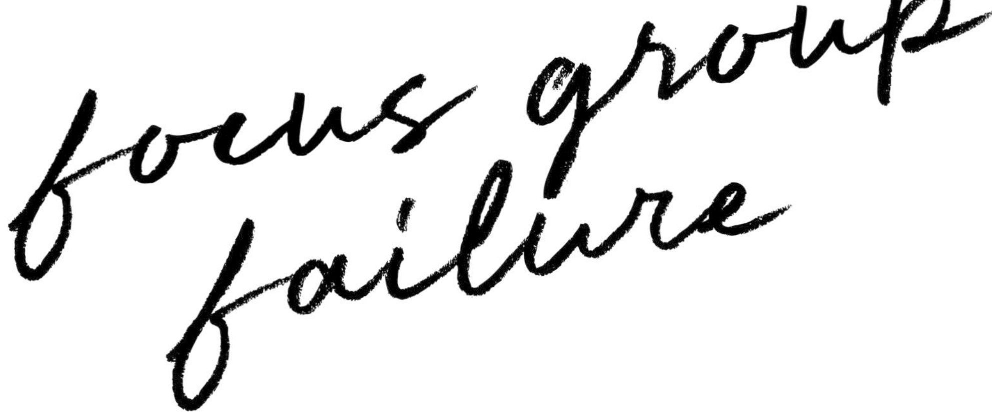

While family's opinions are important, often no one knows you like your friends do. Not every friend has to get along great with your partner, but if *all* your friends are giving them the thumbs-down . . . yikes. Gotta blast!

1 Add the gin, blueberry simple syrup, and lemon juice to a cocktail shaker filled with ice. Shake vigorously.

2 Strain the resulting mixture into a rocks glass filled with ice. Top with club soda.

3 Garnish with the lemon wheel and blueberries.

WANT TO MAKE FLAVORED SIMPLE SYRUPS? It's easier than you may think. To infuse your simple syrup (see page 8) with some extra fruit flavor, just add juice from your fruit of choice during the boiling process.

INGREDIENTS

2 oz. gin

1 oz. Chambord raspberry liqueur

1 oz. lemon juice

2 raspberries, skewered (garnish)

GLASSWARE

Cocktail glass

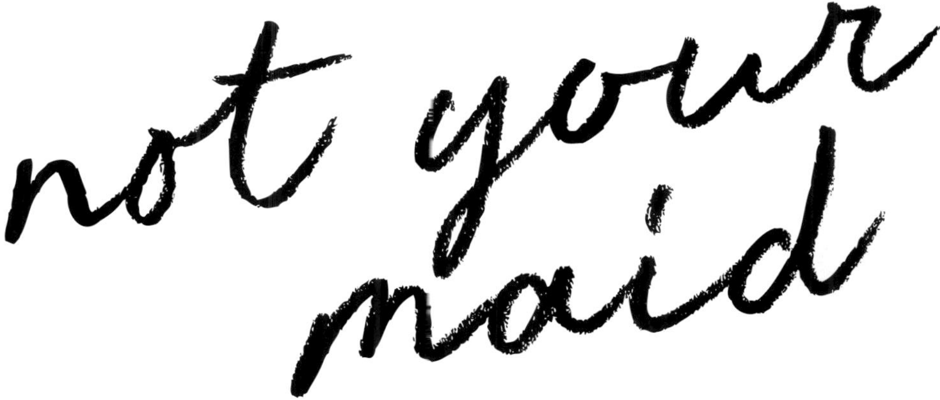

You started out as partners, as equals getting to know each other. Then over time you turned into an employee. How did that happen? You'd think that grown adults would be able to handle doing dishes, washing their clothes, or keeping their personal space moderately tidy. And yet! So when you decide to quit your crappy, severely underpaid job as their personal maid, you can celebrate with this lovely pink concoction.

1 Add gin, Chambord, and lemon juice to a cocktail shaker filled with ice. Shake well.

2 Strain the resulting mixture into a cocktail glass. Garnish with skewered raspberries.

INGREDIENTS

2 oz. gin

⅔ oz. lime juice

⅔ oz. St-Germain Elderflower Liqueur

1 lime wheel (garnish)

GLASSWARE

Cocktail glass

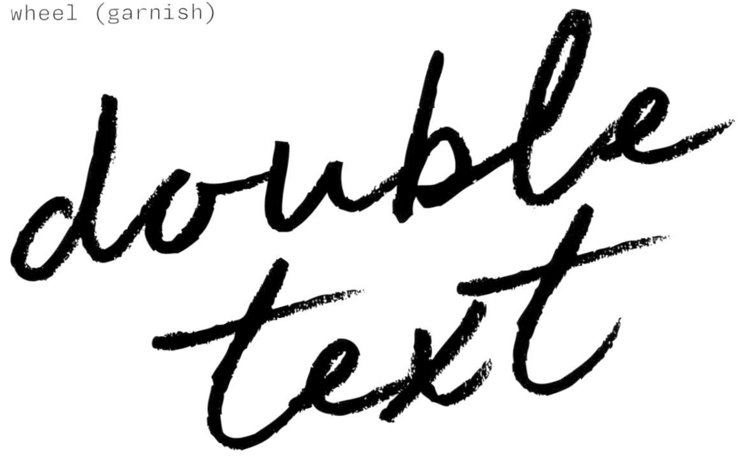

Getting ghosted is obnoxious. But is it more or less obnoxious than someone who texts you all day, every day, regardless of how often you respond? Hard to say. If you've ever been on the receiving end of someone who needed to share their every thought and check in with you constantly, you may just need this modern take on the classic Gimlet.

1 Add the gin, lime juice, and St. Germain to a cocktail shaker filled with ice. Shake well.

2 Strain the resulting mixture into a cocktail glass.

3 Garnish with the lime wheel.

INGREDIENTS

20 mint leaves

3 oz. ginger ale

6 oz. lemonade

3 oz. gin

4 lemon wheels (garnish)

4 mint sprigs (garnish)

GLASSWARE

Highball or pint glasses

spring fling

When things heat up outside, so does the dating game. The problem arises when two people aren't on the same page about whether something beautiful is blooming or if it's just a spring fling. Whether you're looking for a lasting love or even just a little fun, this fizzy ginger ale-and-lemonade concoction is the perfect excuse to host a large gathering. What better way to find what you're seeking? Multiply the recipe to fill a punch bowl with ice, and let guests go to town on this refreshing alternative to boring old fruit punches. It makes four servings!

1 Tear the mint leaves in half and add them to the bottom of a pitcher. Add ice.

2 Pour in the ginger ale, lemonade, and gin, and stir until mixed.

3 Serve in individual glasses and garnish with lemon wheels and mint sprigs.

INGREDIENTS

Salt, for the rim

1 oz. gin

1 oz. grapefruit juice

1 oz. cranberry juice

1 grapefruit wedge (garnish)

GLASSWARE

Rocks glass

magnificently mid

Not every relationship starts—or ends—in an explosion of sparks and fireworks. And while breakups are usually pretty difficult, they aren't always. If you've ever dated someone Magnificently Mid, you'll understand perfectly why this drink may be more of a thrill than that relationship ever was.

1 Wet the rim of a rocks glass and press it into salt.

2 Add the gin, grapefruit juice, and cranberry juice to a cocktail shaker filled with ice. Shake vigorously.

3 Strain the resulting mixture over ice into a rocks glass (or highball glass if you're extra thirsty).

4 Garnish with the grapefruit wedge.

INGREDIENTS

1 oz. gin

1 oz. cranberry juice

1 splash triple sec

½ lime (juiced)

1 lime wheel (garnish)

GLASSWARE

Rocks glass

unfashionably late

Stuff happens. Cars break down, family emergencies come up, traffic's a nightmare. Just about everyone has had to send a "sorry I'm going to be a bit late" text. But if you find yourself dating someone who sends that text before every single date, or worse, even before important events, it stops looking like bad luck and starts looking like a bad choice of partner.

1 Add the gin, cranberry juice, triple sec, and lime juice to a cocktail shaker filled with ice and shake vigorously.

2 Strain the resulting mixture into a rocks glass containing your desired amount of ice.

3 Garnish with the lime wheel.

INGREDIENTS

2 oz. gin

2 oz. club soda

1 splash grenadine

1 maraschino cherry (garnish)

GLASSWARE

Rocks glass

It's important to have friends and to continue making time for those people after getting in a relationship. But if you've been together a while and you're still continuously getting blown off in favor of your partner's pals, it may be time to reassess. Enjoy your weekends without stressing about whether they'll bother coming home with this simple, delicious sipper.

1 Add ice to a rocks glass and pour in the gin and club soda.

2 Stir thoroughly.

3 Top with grenadine.

4 Garnish with the maraschino cherry.

INGREDIENTS

1 oz. gin

1 oz. Campari

1 oz. freshly squeezed orange juice

1 orange wedge (garnish)

GLASSWARE

Rocks glass

We've all heard the fairy tales of "I saw them and I just knew." But few of us have ever just "known" right away. That being said, after some time together, it should be pretty clear how you feel and where you're headed. And if you're years in with someone who refuses to commit because they're still "just not sure," it's time to leave them sitting on that fence so you can seek greener pastures.

1 Add the gin, Campari, and orange juice to a cocktail shaker filled with ice. Shake well.

2 Strain the resulting mixture into a rocks glass filled with ice.

3 Garnish with the orange wedge.

INGREDIENTS

1 oz. gin

1 oz. cherry liqueur

1 oz. lemon juice

1 splash simple syrup
(see page 8)

1 maraschino cherry
(garnish)

1 orange slice (garnish)

GLASSWARE

Rocks glass

We've all seen the romance books out there about the rakish duke finally being tamed by a beautiful woman, where he completely forgets about other women and devotes himself entirely to her. Unfortunately, in the real world, the player you picked usually just turns out to be . . . a player. Enjoy this tasty sour cocktail in honor of the Most Valuable Player that you no longer want on your team.

1 Add the gin, cherry liqueur, lemon juice, and simple syrup to a cocktail shaker filled with ice and shake well.

2 Strain the resulting mixture into a rocks glass filled with ice.

3 Garnish with the maraschino cherry and orange slice.

INGREDIENTS

1½ oz. gin

⅔ oz. cherry liqueur

⅔ oz. triple sec

2 oz. pineapple juice

1 maraschino cherry (garnish)

1 pineapple wedge (garrish)

GLASSWARE

Hurricane glass

trust your gut

We've all been there. Something went sideways, and we thought, *I knew I had a bad feeling about this*. It's hard when your gut and your head—or even worse, your gut and your *heart*—are telling you two different things. At least it's a good reminder that sometimes all you need to do is listen to your instincts.

1 Pour the gin, liqueur, triple sec, and pineapple juice into a cocktail shaker filled with ice and shake vigorously.

2 Strain the resulting mixture into a hurricane glass filled with ice.

3 Garnish with maraschino cherry and pineapple wedge.

INGREDIENTS

1 oz. gin

1 tsp. sugar

1 splash lemon juice

2 oz. club soda

1 orange wheel (garnish)

1 maraschino cherry (garnish)

GLASSWARE

Collins glass or highball glass

Good relationships are built on trust. Not-so-good relationships are built on not-so-good building blocks. And when your foundation is flimsy, it's easy for something simple and seemingly insignificant to knock the whole thing over. This is the perfect drink to enjoy when it all falls down.

1 Add the gin, sugar, and lemon juice to a cocktail shaker filled with ice and shake until thoroughly mixed.

2 Strain the resulting mixture into a collins or highball glass. Top with club soda.

3 Garnish with the orange wheel and maraschino cherry.

VARIATION

As there are Tom Collins recipes that use lemon or lime juice, feel free to use the one you prefer. Only have lime juice? No worries. The flavors are slightly different but equally tasty.

INGREDIENTS

1 splash triple sec

2 mint leaves

1 oz. gin

2 oz. cranberry juice

1 mint sprig (garnish)

GLASSWARE

Rocks glass

Going on a first date is one of the scariest things that's considered normal and standard in adult life. There are some real psychos out there. And, even more common, some real jerks. If you've ever been on a date where you asked for the check as early as possible just to get out of there, enjoy this cocktail in lieu of the dessert you would have enjoyed with better company.

1 Muddle the mint leaves and the triple sec at the bottom of a cocktail shaker.

2 Add ice to the shaker and add the gin and cranberry juice. Shake well.

3 Strain the resulting mixture into a rocks glass. Garnish with the mint sprig.

INGREDIENTS

2 oz. Hendrick's gin

⅔ oz. lavender liqueur

⅔ oz. club soda

1 lavender sprig (garnish)

GLASSWARE

Cocktail glass

pride and prejudice

While the name of this cocktail may call to mind a terribly romantic book, it's also representative of two of the most difficult personality traits to deal with in a partner. When you think you've found your Mr. Darcy, but he turns out to be a Mr. Wickham, this flavorful and aromatic cocktail will help you deal with the disappointment.

1 Add the gin and lavender liqueur to a cocktail shaker filled with ice. Shake well.

2 Strain the resulting mixture into a cocktail glass. Top with club soda.

3 Garnish with the lavender sprig.

Blindside, page 180

WHIS-KEY YOUR CAR

This chapter is a tribute to the smooth-talking charmers and fiery exits that left you with aching heads and heavier hearts. Each cocktail pays homage to the complexity of bourbon, rye, and scotch—as layered as the mistakes you'll never make again.

INGREDIENTS

1½ oz. Four Roses Bourbon

1 lemon (juiced)

1 teaspoon sugar

Club soda

1 lemon rind (garnish)

Maraschino cherries (garnish)

GLASSWARE

Highball glass

There are topics that are sensitive by nature, but some people take this to an explosive new level. We've all found ourselves tiptoeing around difficult conversations or avoiding subjects that were previously the cause of an argument. But if you miscalculated and everything blew up, it's time to retreat and enjoy this Tom Collins-inspired cocktail from Four Roses.

1 Pour a jigger of Four Roses into a tall glass over cubed ice.

2 Add the juice of one lemon, followed by sugar, to the drink. Fill with club soda and stir.

3 Garnish with lemon rind and cherries.

INGREDIENTS

2 oz. Jim Beam Bourbon

⅔ oz. sweet vermouth

2 drops bitters

1 maraschino cherry (garnish)

GLASSWARE

Rocks glass

When you're single for a while, it's easy to get used to functioning solo. You don't have to do much to consider others in your everyday life. But this usually does—and should—change when you get into a relationship. This simple Manhattan is inspired by the people who simply can't make the transition and therefore should keep focusing on what matters to them most: themselves.

1 Fill a mixing glass with ice and add the bourbon, vermouth, and bitters. Stir gently to avoid bruising the drink.

2 Strain the mixture over ice into a rocks glass. Garnish with the maraschino cherry.

INGREDIENTS

2 oz. bourbon

¾ oz. simple syrup (see page 8)

¾ oz. lemon juice

1 egg white

1 lemon peel (garnish)

GLASSWARE

Rocks glass

One of the best things about being in a good relationship is feeling totally safe to be your unfiltered self. But if you have a partner with very little patience, you can find yourself overstressing about everything you say and do in an effort not to piss them off. That's no way to live. This sour cocktail, courtesy of Hartfield & Co. Bourbon, includes an egg white for when you're sick of Walking on Eggshells.

1 Build the drink in a shaker, dry shake (without ice), add ice, and shake again.

2 Double strain the drink into a double rocks glass over fresh ice.

3 Express oil from the lemon peel over the drink, garnish with the lemon peel, and serve.

INGREDIENTS

4 mint leaves

1 teaspoon powdered sugar

1 splash water

2 oz. Maker's Mark

1 mint sprig (garnish)

GLASSWARE

Rocks glass

Okay, most of the drinks in this book are characterized by pretty specific grievances. Cheating, irresponsibility, laziness. But this one is, by nature, undefinable. Sometimes the vibes are just off. Even if you can't put your finger on what it is, the vibes don't lie. Curate a better environment for yourself with this delectable mint julep treat.

1 Tear the mint leaves in half to release their flavor, then muddle in the bottom of your glass with powdered sugar and water.

2 Fill the glass with cracked ice, then add the bourbon. Stir gently.

3 Garnish with the mint sprig.

INGREDIENTS

1¼ oz. rye whiskey

¾ oz. sweet vermouth

½ oz. Domaine de Canton

1 dash Angostura Bitters

1 strip lemon peel (garnish)

GLASSWARE

Rocks glass

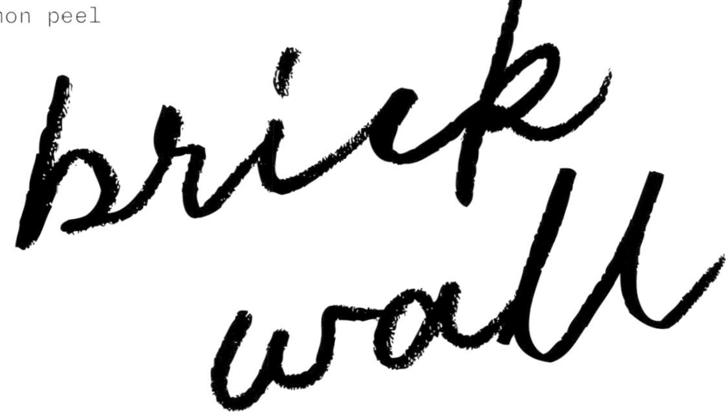

"My way or the highway" is a mentality that most people outgrow once they're no longer of an age where temper tantrums are socially acceptable. But there is that rare outlier who simply never learned that there are perspectives other than their own. This rye cocktail is created in spite of the most stubborn among us; we all hope never to encounter you in the dating field.

1 Chill a rocks glass in the freezer.

2 Add the rye, vermouth, Domaine de Canton, and bitters to a mixing glass, fill it two-thirds of the way with ice, and stir until chilled.

3 Strain into the chilled glass over ice and garnish with the strip of lemon peel.

INGREDIENTS

2 oz. bourbon

1 oz. POM Wonderful pomegranate juice

½ oz. honey

½ oz. lemon juice

Pomegranate seeds (garnish)

GLASSWARE

Rocks glass

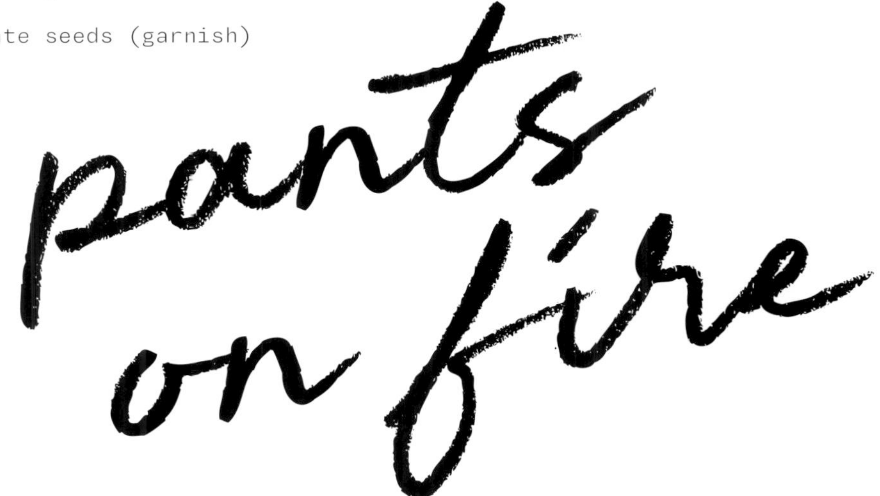

You'd think that after seeing thousands of examples—in stories, movies, the news, and so on—it would be obvious that lying often comes back to bite you much worse than if you'd just been honest in the first place. Some people never learn.

1 Place the cocktail ingredients, except for the garnish, in a cocktail shaker, fill it two-thirds of the way with ice, and shake until chilled.

2 Strain over ice into a rocks glass and garnish with the pomegranate seeds.

INGREDIENTS

1 oz. simple syrup (see page 8)

3 to 4 shakes bitters

2 oz. Willett Family Estate Bottled Rye

Water or club soda (optional)

Maraschino cherries (garnish)

Orange wheel (garnish)

GLASSWARE

Rocks glass

Whether you believe in love at first sight or not, some social norms really shouldn't be broken. Talking about the children you'll raise together after appetizers on date one. Proposing on the second date. Slow *way* down with this relaxing sipper.

1 Combine simple syrup and bitters in a rocks glass. Top with ice and fill with rye. Leave a little room for water or club soda if desired.

2 Garnish with one or two maraschino cherries and rub the orange wheel around the rim of the glass. Enjoy!

INGREDIENTS

1½ oz. X by Glenmorangie single malt scotch whisky

¾ oz. Lustau Fino Jarana sherry

¾ oz. chamomile syrup

½ oz. lemon juice

1 dehydrated lemon wheel (garnish)

GLASSWARE

Coupe

This recipe is for those who are simply done. You burned the candle at both ends, or the passion burned bright, and now the fire has consumed everything and nothing is left. When there's nothing left to salvage, there's nothing to do but start over. Why not start with this single malt Scotch cocktail?

1 Place the cocktail ingredients , except for the garnish, in a cocktail shaker, fill it two-thirds of the way with ice, and shake until chilled.

2 Strain the cocktail into the coupe and garnish with the dehydrated lemon wheel.

INGREDIENTS

2 mint leaves

1 splash lime juice

2 oz. bourbon whiskey

1 oz. ginger ale

1 lime wedge (garnish)

1 mint leaf (garnish)

GLASSWARE

Rocks glass

big spender

There's nothing wrong with splurging from time to time. But if you've ever dated someone who has no idea how to manage or save their money, you'll know that some people never learned impulse control. Good on you for dodging that bullet. Enjoy this cocktail in honor of the retirement you'll get to have in the absence of a partner who wastes all your money.

1 Muddle the mint leaves and lime juice in the bottom of a cocktail shaker.

2 Fill the cocktail shaker with ice and add the bourbon. Shake well.

3 Strain the resulting mixture into a rocks glass filled with ice.

4 Top with ginger ale. Lightly stir if desired.

5 Garnish with the lime wedge and mint leaf.

INGREDIENTS

2 blackberries

6 to 8 mint leaves

½ oz. honey syrup (equal parts honey and hot water)

1 oz. lemon juice

3 oz. bourbon

Soda water, to finish

Blackberries (garnish)

1 mint sprig (garnish)

GLASSWARE

Rocks glass

Everyone goes through rough patches, but there's a difference between a rough patch and constant rough terrain. It is unbelievably tough to start dating someone who not only hasn't gotten it together yet, but also seems to be actively falling apart at the seams. Cheers to you for passing up that additional full-time job.

1 Muddle 2 blackberries and the mint leaves with honey syrup in cocktail shaker.

2 Add lemon juice and bourbon to cocktail shaker. Shake vigorously with cracked ice.

3 Double-strain into rocks glass with fresh crushed ice.

4 Top with soda water and garnish with blackberries and mint sprig.

INGREDIENTS

2 oz. The Famous Grouse Blended Scotch Whisky

¾ oz. simple syrup (see page 8)

¾ oz. lemon juice

¼ oz. dry red wine

1 lemon slice (garnish)

1 brandy-soaked cherry (garnish)

GLASSWARE

Rocks glass

worlds collide

Opposites attract. Many of us can think of couples for whom this is absolutely true. But sometimes opposites are just too opposite. When Worlds Collide, either they learn to live in harmony or everything gets destroyed. If you own this book, we can guess which happened to you.

1 Place the Scotch, simple syrup, and lemon juice in a cocktail shaker, fill it two-thirds of the way with ice, and shake until chilled.

2 Strain into a rocks glass filled with ice and float the wine on top by pouring it over the back of a spoon.

3 Garnish with the lemon slice and brandy-soaked cherry.

INGREDIENTS

1 rosemary sprig

1½ oz. honey syrup (equal parts honey and hot water)

1 oz. rye whiskey

1½ oz. lemon juice

1 oz. egg white

1 rosemary sprig (garnish)

GLASSWARE

Rocks glass

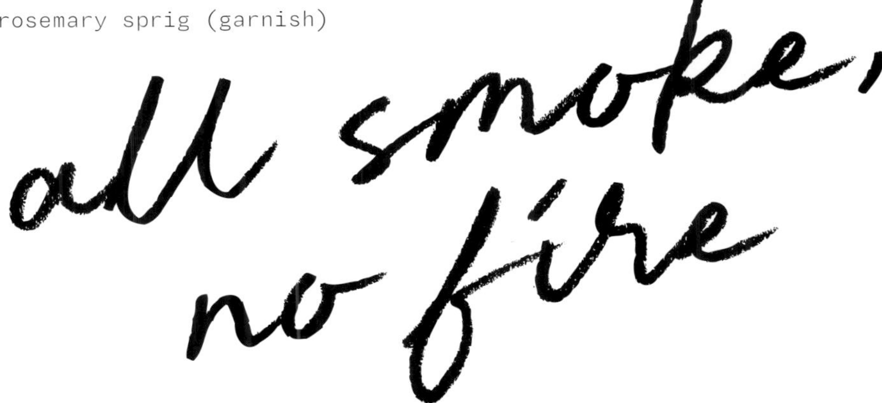

You have a great time together. It's so much fun. But there is simply nothing underneath it. Fun is fun, but it can only support a relationship for so long. It's a shame when someone you get along with just doesn't connect with you on a deeper level, but hey, nothing wrong with having a good time. And there's no good time as tasty as this cocktail!

1 Muddle the rosemary sprig and honey syrup in a shaker.

2 Add the liquid ingredients and egg white and dry shake (without ice).

3 Add ice and shake again before straining into a rocks glass. Garnish with the rosemary sprig and enjoy!

INGREDIENTS

¼ oz. cold brew coffee concentrate

1½ oz. bourbon

Mexican Coke, as needed

1 lemon peel, expressed

GLASSWARE

Sour glass

When things are going really well and then someone ends it out of the blue, it's almost so shocking and confusing that it takes a second to feel anything but . . . "huh?" Once you get around to dealing with your (very justified) anger and sadness, this pick-me-up coffee cocktail is there to jump-start your healing journey. Although it can be made with any cola, we love Mexican Coke (it's made with real cane sugar). We also recommend using Maker's Mark bourbon.

1 Fill a glass with ice and add the coffee and bourbon.

2 Gently stir until chilled. Top with Mexican Coke and finish with oil from a strip of lemon peel.

INGREDIENTS

1 splash simple syrup (see page 8)

1 orange peel strip

2 drops bitters

2 oz. Maker's Mark

Club soda (optional)

Lemon peel (garnish)

GLASSWARE

Rocks glass

Being with someone who loves their job is often a good thing. It's hard to find employment that is fulfilling, and having a partner who is passionate about what they do can be wonderful. But if that work keeps coming before you, then you need to get your priorities in order—since they're clearly incapable. This drink is for the ones left behind by the workaholics.

1 Add the simple syrup to a rocks glass and drop in a strip of orange peel. Add the bitters and muddle together.

2 Fill the glass with ice, then add your bourbon. Stir together slowly. Add club soda if desired.

3 Garnish with the lemon peel.

INGREDIENTS

1 oz. Tennessee whiskey

1 oz. peach purée

Champagne

GLASSWARE

Coupe

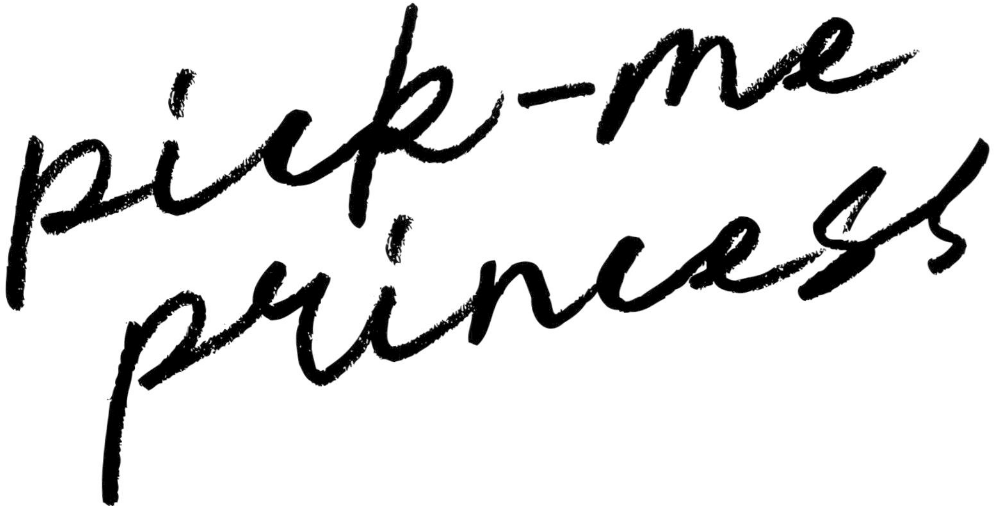

It's natural to want to be liked by others. Especially when it's your friends and family, people whose opinions matter to you, it makes sense that your partner would do their best to befriend everyone. But when they try a little too hard to cozy up to others, or when they try to make themselves seem more appealing by putting someone else down, then it may be your sign to let someone else pick that Pick-Me Princess and pick up this cocktail instead.

1 Combine whiskey and peach purée in a glass.

2 Top off the drink with champagne.

Just Ignore It, page 208

SOBER ENOUGH TO SEE YOU CLEARLY

After all the heartbreaks, the messy nights, and questionable pairings, we end with clarity. Each mocktail offers a chance to taste something clean, reflective, and perfectly balanced, much like finding the courage to move on. This chapter is your toast to closure, with drinks as bright and refreshing as this new chapter of your life.

INGREDIENTS

1 sugar cube

1 oz. lemon juice

4 oz. ginger ale

1 lemon twist (garnish)

GLASSWARE

Champagne flute

mr. right-all-the-time

We're all looking for Mr. or Mrs. Right. Right? But when the person we've found is seemingly incapable of being wrong, then it must mean you are. And you know what? That might be the one thing they're actually right about—because you were definitely wrong to ever date them.

1 Place a sugar cube at the bottom of a champagne flute.

2 Add the lemon juice, then the ginger ale.

3 Garnish with the twist of lemon.

INGREDIENTS

3 oz. iced tea (any variety, though best if made fresh)

1 oz. tonic water

1 splash lemon juice

1 lemon peel (garnish)

1 mint sprig (garnish)

GLASSWARE

Highball glass

Opening up to people is hard. Letting down your guard, letting someone in—it's seriously scary stuff. But being with someone means being yourself, even in the ways that are uncomfortable or difficult. And if you've spent years with someone who refuses to let down their guard for even a moment, it becomes difficult to trust someone who doesn't seem to trust you. So here's to being unapologetically yourself and finding someone who can offer you the same!

1 Steep your favorite tea in boiling water, then set aside to cool. If using premade iced tea, skip this step.

2 Add the iced tea to a highball glass filled with ice. Add the tonic water and lemon juice and stir together gently.

3 Garnish with the lemon peel and mint sprig.

INGREDIENTS

2 oz. peach nectar

2 oz. ginger ale or sparkling cider

1 peach wedge (garnish)

GLASSWARE

Champagne flute

Money isn't everything, but finding someone responsible enough to share financial responsibilities with is no trivial matter. And if you've dated someone who treats money like it's a game—or turns every game into a betting opportunity—you need to find someone who has heard of the term *risk management*.

1 Fill a champagne flute with the peach nectar.

2 Top with ginger ale or sparkling cider. Stir gently to combine.

3 Garnish with the peach wedge.

INGREDIENTS

2 oz. pink lemonade

1 oz. lime juice

1 oz. club soda

1 lime wheel (garnish)

Fresh herbs (garnish)

Edible flowers (garnish)

GLASSWARE

Rocks glass

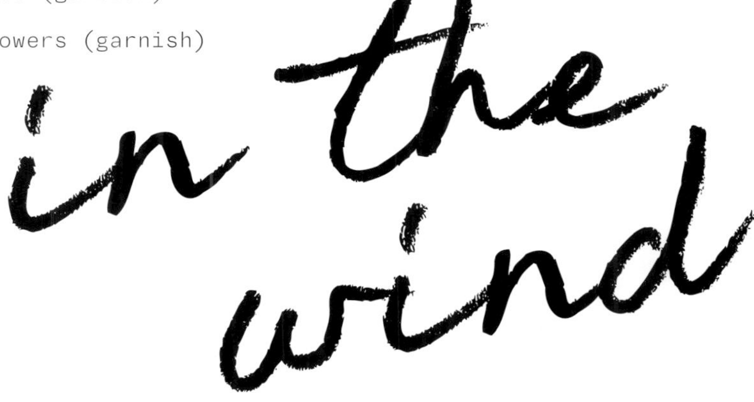

There's a difference between being Ghosted (see page 87) and dating someone who is seemingly unreachable. Most of us have gotten a little too attached to our phones, it's true, but going for days at a time without checking your phone when you have people who care for you trying to contact you reads more "callous and indifferent" than "zen and disconnected." Disconnect from them with this fresh and colorful mocktail.

1 Add pink lemonade and lime juice to a cocktail shaker filled with ice. Shake well.

2 Strain the resulting mixture into a rocks glass and top with club soda.

3 Garnish with the lime wheel, fresh herbs, and edible flowers. (Thyme and rosemary make particularly aromatic additions!)

INGREDIENTS

1 oz. ginger ale

2 oz. seltzer (any flavor)

Raspberries (garnish)

GLASSWARE

Champagne flute

fizzle

Things can start out hot and the passion can burn brightly, but all too often, it just . . . fizzles. Being with someone for a long time can make it hard to keep the spark alive, but if it truly goes out and nothing will bring it back, that's that. You deserve fireworks that last!

1. Pour the ginger ale and seltzer into a champagne flute.
2. Drop in fresh raspberries as garnish.

INGREDIENTS

1 oz. coconut cream

3 oz. pineapple juice

2 to 4 cups crushed ice

4 pineapple slices (garnish)

4 maraschino cherries (garnish)

GLASSWARE

Wine glass

You are a great time. Just by owning this book, you've proved that. So why would you date someone who dims your sparkle? Life is too short to spend it with people who rain on your parade. Spend your time with people who lift you up with this delicious virgin Piña Colada recipe meant for four.

1 Add coconut cream, pineapple juice, and ice to the blender and blend until smooth. Add as much ice as you want until you reach your desired consistency. It doesn't need to be too thick; when the ice melts, you don't want to leave yourself with a watered-down drink.

2 Pour into individual wine glasses and garnish with pineapple slices and cherries.

INGREDIENTS

4 oranges (3 juiced, 1 peeled and thinly sliced)

12 oz. grape juice

6 oz. apple juice

2 oz. lemon juice

GLASSWARE

Pitcher or punch bowl

sloppy joe

We try not to be too judgy, but come on. You can have a day (or even a few) where you're not all put together, but being a slob all the time is just embarrassing. And dating a slob might feel even worse. But you'll feel better after drinking this delicious fruity treat of a drink, which makes 4 to 6 servings.

1 Juice three oranges into a large, sealable container. Peel and slice the other orange, and put those slices into the same container.

2 Add the grape juice, apple juice, and lemon juice.

3 Seal the container and refrigerate for 24 hours.

4 Pour into a pitcher or punch bowl.

INGREDIENTS

Salt, for the rim

1 oz. lemon juice

1 oz. lime juice

1 oz. orange juice

1 oz. simple syrup (see page 8)

1 lime slice and peel (garnish)

GLASSWARE

Margarita glass

We tend to assume that other people have rich inner lives we just aren't privy to. And a lot of times that's true! But some people . . . there's just not that much there. If you've ever tried to dive into a deep conversation only to realize you were in a kiddie pool, this mocktail is for you.

1 Rub the lime along the rim of your Margarita glass and rim it with salt.

2 Add the lemon juice, lime juice, orange juice, and simple syrup to a cocktail shaker filled with ice and shake until combined.

3 Add ice to your Margarita glass and strain the contents of the cocktail shaker into it. Garnish with the lime slice and peels. For a Frozen Virgin Margarita, add about a cup of ice (give or take, depending on how thick you want it to be) and blend.

INGREDIENTS

1 oz. iced tea (unsweetened)

1 oz. lemonade

1 oz. cola

Lemon wheels (garnish)

GLASSWARE

Highball glass

the conductor

Few things and more frustrating than being micromanaged. It's one thing at work, but if you've ever been micromanaged in your personal life, you know it's so much worse. Imagine your boss also having an opinion about what you wear to the gym. When you need to cool off from the justifiable anger this triggers in you, this refreshing drink is here for you.

1 Add the ingredients together in your glass. Stir until mixed.

2 Garnish with the lemon wheels.

INGREDIENTS

1 glass orange juice

1 splash grenadine

1 orange wheel (garnish)

GLASSWARE

Collins glass

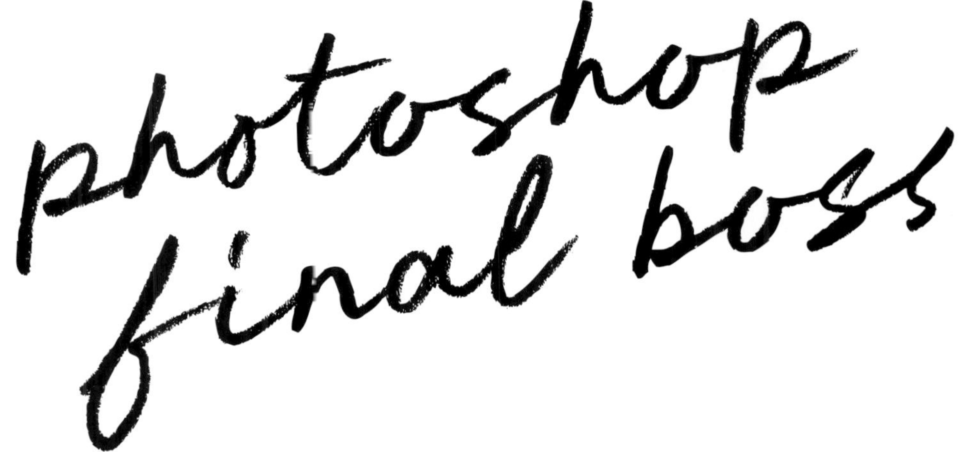

Of course you're not going to post photos where you're looking your worst. But there's a difference between putting your best foot forward and digitally altering yourself into oblivion. And if you've ever gone to meet up with someone you literally could not recognize in person based their photos . . . well, enjoying this drink is always a beautiful alternative to an evening wasted on someone who can't be themselves.

1 Add orange juice to a glass filled with ice.

2 Top with a splash of grenadine.

3 Garnish with the orange wheel.

INGREDIENTS

½ lime (juiced)

1 oz. coconut syrup

8 oz. cola

Lime wedges (garnish)

GLASSWARE

Highball glass

just ignore it

Problems have to be dealt with. Sadly, very few problems of real significance go away on their own. And if those put-off problems pile up, one day you'll find yourself looking at one big, insurmountable issue. Sometimes all it takes to make a mountain out of a molehill is just a lot of molehills.

1 Squeeze the lime juice into your glass.

2 Add ice, then add the coconut syrup and cola. Stir until mixed.

3 Garnish with the lime wedges.

INGREDIENTS

2 oz. orange juice

2 oz. Sprite

1 orange slice (garnish)

GLASSWARE

Champagne flute

Few traits are as important as dependability when considering the kind of person you want to spend your life with. You need someone you can call on when things get ugly, when you need help, or simply when you need to not be alone. And some people aren't ready for that responsibility. So if you've dated someone who was about as supportive as a wet paper towel, let this bubbly drink help kick-start your journey to finding someone you can rely on.

1 Fill your champagne flute halfway with orange juice.

2 Top off with Sprite and stir together.

3 Garnish with the orange slice.

VARIATION

Sprite not your thing? Try it with ginger ale instead!

INGREDIENTS

8 oz. tomato juice

1 dash Worcestershire sauce

1 dash lemon juice

1 dash pepper

Garnish with anything your heart desires

GLASSWARE

Pint glass

j'accuse!

Dating someone who's insanely jealous for no reason is like dating an amateur detective who moonlights as a conspiracy theorist. It takes nothing to make them think you're cheating on them, or lying to them, or betraying them in any number of ways. So when you're tired of being treated like a criminal, whip up this tasty drink and greet the day as a free person.

1 Add ice to your glass, then fill with tomato juice.

2 Add a dash of Worcestershire sauce, lemon juice, and black pepper. Stir thoroughly.

3 Garnish with anything you please.

VARIATION

This is just the base for a successful Virgin Bloody Mary. If you'd like to add other common ingredients you happen to have lying around (like horseradish or salt, for example), you can easily build off this recipe.

INGREDIENTS

4 oz. black tea (hot)

½ oz heavy whipping cream

1 tsp. sugar

1 dash cocoa powder

1 oz. milk (frothed)

1 dash pumpkin pie spice (garnish)

GLASSWARE

Mug

"Cheater, cheater, pumpkin eater." Doesn't seem fair—they cheat *and* they get to have a pumpkin treat? I don't think so. It's your turn to enjoy a pumpkin-flavored libation.

1 Fill a mug about two-thirds of way with hot black tea.

2 Add the heavy whipping cream, sugar, and cocoa powder and mix in.

3 Top with frothed milk.

4 Garnish with a dash of pumpkin pie spice.

METRIC CONVERSIONS

US Measurement	Approximate Metric Liquid Measurement	Approximate Metric Dry Measurement
1 teaspoon	5 ml	5 g
1 tablespoon or ½ ounce	15 ml	14 g
1 ounce or ⅛ cup	30 ml	29 g
¼ cup or 2 ounces	60 ml	57 g
⅓ cup	80 ml	76 g
½ cup or 4 ounces	120 ml	113 g
⅔ cup	160 ml	151 g
¾ cup or 6 ounces	180 ml	170 g
1 cup or 8 ounces or ½ pint	240 ml	227 g
1½ cups or 12 ounces	350 ml	340 g
2 cups or 1 pint or 16 ounces	475 ml	454 g
3 cups or 1½ pints	700 ml	680 g
4 cups or 2 pints or 1 quart	950 ml	908 g

INDEX

ABOUT CIDER MILL PRESS BOOK PUBLISHERS

Cider Mill Press publishes exceptional books that combine creativity and craftsmanship. As an imprint of HarperCollins Focus, we specialize in premium cookbooks, cocktail and spirits guides, and illustrated gift books, all distinguished by compelling content, striking design, and a commitment to quality in every detail. Cider Mill Press sets the standard for books that inform, inspire, and elevate everyday moments. Learn more at cidermillpress.com.

"Where Good Books Are Ready for Press"

501 Nelson Place
Nashville, Tennessee 37214